W9-DCE-984

Alfred Noble Library
32901 Plymouth Road
Livonia, MI 48150-1793
{734}421-6600

Great Empires

The British Empire

ELLIS ROXBURGH

Alfred Noble Library
32901 Plymouth Road
Livonia, MI 48150-1793
{734}421-6600

Cavendish
Square

New York

SEP 2 2 2016

3 9082 12765 4690

Published in 2016 by Cavendish Square Publishing, LLC
243 5th Avenue, Suite 136, New York, NY 10016

© 2016 Brown Bear Books Ltd

First Edition

Website: cavendishsq.com

This publication represents the opinions and views of the author based on his or her personal experiences, knowledge, and research. The information in this book serves as a general guide only. the author and publisher have used their best efforts in preparing this book and disclaim liability rising directly or indirectly from the use and application of this book.

CPSIA Compliance Information: Batch #WS15CSQ

Library of Congress Cataloging-in-Publication Data

Roxburgh, Ellis.
The British Empire / Ellis Roxburgh.
pages cm. — (Great empires)
Includes bibliographical references and index.
ISBN 978-1-50260-634-1 (hardcover) ISBN 978-1-50260-635-8 (ebook)
1. Great Britain—Colonies—History—20th century—Juvenile literature.
2. Postcolonialism—Commonwealth countries—Juvenile literature.
3. Decolonization—History—20th century—Juvenile literature.
4. Commonwealth countries—History—Juvenile literature. I. Title.

DA16.R69 2016
909'.0971941—dc23
2015008487

For Brown Bear Books Ltd:
Editorial Director: Lindsey Lowe
Managing Editor: Tim Cooke
Children's Publisher: Anne O'Daly
Design Manager: Keith Davis
Designer: Melissa Roskell
Picture Manager: Sophie Mortimer

Picture Credits:
Front Cover: Shutterstock: Chris Pole br; Thinkstock: iStock main.
Getty Images: Popperfoto 32; Library of Congress: 9, 12, 13, 14, 15, 25, 33; Mary Evans Picture Library: 4;
Robert Hunt Library: 1, 7tl, 11, 16, 18, 20, 21, 22, 23, 24, 27, 28, 29, 31, 37, 39, 40, 41, 42; Royal Naval Air Squadron: 43;
Shutterstock: Claudio Divizia 5, T Photography 38; Thinkstock: iStock 34, 35, 36, Amanda Lewis 17, Photos.com 19, 26, 30;
TopFoto: Granger Collection 8, 10.
Artistic Effects: Shutterstock.

All other artwork and maps Brown Bear Books

Brown Bear Books has made every attempt to contact the copyright holder.
If you have any information please contact licensing@brownbearbooks.co.uk

All rights reserved. No part of this book may be reproduced, stored in a retrieval system, or transmitted in any form or by any means, electronic, mechanical, photocopying, recording, or otherwise, without the prior written permission of the copyright holder.

Manufactured in the United States of America

CONTENTS

Introduction

At its peak in the early 1900s, the British Empire ruled a quarter of the world's population—around 458 million people.

By the end of the nineteenth century, the small nation of Great Britain off the coast of northwestern Europe had created what was commonly called "the empire on which the sun never sets." British territory was spread so widely across the globe that it was always daylight somewhere, even if it was the middle of the night in

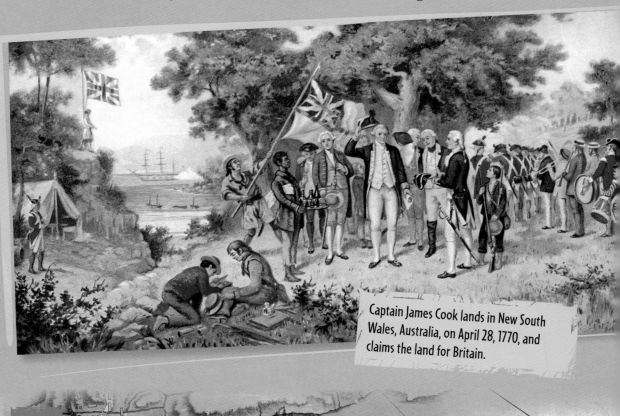

Captain James Cook lands in New South Wales, Australia, on April 28, 1770, and claims the land for Britain.

London, the **imperial** capital city. Building the empire had taken Britain nearly three hundred years. During that time, it had gained and then lost **colonies** along virtually the whole of the eastern coast of North America but had gone on to establish major colonies in Canada, Australia, New Zealand, South Africa, and India.

Britain also had dozens more smaller colonies around the world. Many were originally bases for the Royal Navy. The Navy controlled the world's oceans from the early eighteenth century to the early twentieth century.

The Palace of Westminster was built during the mid-nineteenth century to house the British government.

Troops of the Australian and New Zealand Army Corps (ANZAC) charge the Turkish lines at Gallipoli during World War I (1914–1918).

Pacific Ocean

CAN

Key

The British Empire ca. 191

As Britain's national song, or anthem, claimed, Britannia ruled the waves. The powerful Royal Navy protected British merchants and vessels around the world, allowing the British to build an empire based on trade. The colonies supplied resources for Britain's factories, and supplied a market for British **manufactures**, such as textiles produced by British cotton mills. The British Army and the Indian Army ensured that no one could challenge Britain's power or damage its **strategic** dominance anywhere in the world.

The British Empire

UNITED
KINGDOM

WEST
INDIES

*Atlantic
Ocean*

INDIA

Pacific Ocean

Indian Ocean

SOUTH
AFRICA

AUSTRALIA

NEW ZEALAND

After World War I (1914–1918), the power of the British empire's navy and army began to decline. The decline continued after World War II (1939–1945). The British could no longer afford to police an empire. As its colonies achieved independence, Britain invited them to become part of a new organization, the Commonwealth—but this time as equals rather than subjects.

The Roots of the Empire

The British began their rise to imperial dominance slowly. Other European powers, particularly Spain, Portugal, and the Netherlands, led the way in seizing overseas territory.

The origins of the British Empire date back long before Great Britain was created in 1707 by the union of England and Scotland. In 1496, King Henry VII of England (ruled 1485–1509) gave John Cabot, an Italian navigator and explorer, permission to sail across the Atlantic Ocean on behalf of England. He was trying to discover a direct sea route to the rich lands of Asia and claim new lands for England.

On June 24, 1497, Cabot landed on what he took to be Asia. It was in fact the coast of what is now Canada in North America. Cabot named the land "New-found-land" and claimed it in the name of Henry VII.

Catching Up

Christopher Columbus had already reached the Americas in 1492 and two years later, in 1494, the Spanish and Portuguese divided the "New World" between them in

In this nineteenth-century engraving, John Cabot claims Newfoundland on behalf of the English king in 1497.

an agreement called the Treaty of Tordesillas. With the discovery of gold and silver in Mexico, Peru, and Bolivia, the Spanish monarchy had great wealth to spend on acquiring territory. Meanwhile, the Portuguese explored the coast of Africa, and reached India and Brazil. They controlled the valuable spice market.

The English were jealous of their European rivals' wealth and territory. Henry VIII (ruled 1509–1547) removed England from the authority of the Catholic Church and set up an English Protestant Church. Many English people now believed the king had a duty to form an overseas empire to spread the Protestant faith, just as the Spanish monarchs were spreading Catholicism in the New World.

KEY PEOPLE

John Cabot

Although he was born in Venice, Italy, John Cabot (circa 1450–ca. 1499) worked for the English king, Henry VII. Just as the Spanish monarchs sponsored Christopher Columbus, Henry paid Cabot to discover new lands. After an unsuccessful first voyage, Cabot set out in 1497 to find a westward sea route to Asia and its valuable spices but instead discovered Newfoundland. On his third voyage, seeking a westward route to Japan, Cabot and his ship disappeared.

English colonies in the West Indies became rich by growing sugar on plantations like this one painted in Jamaica in the nineteenth century.

Sir Walter Raleigh (front) captures the governor of Trinidad during a raid on the Spanish Caribbean colony.

KEY PEOPLE

Sir Walter Raleigh

A favorite of Queen Elizabeth I (ruled 1558–1603), Walter Raleigh is said to have introduced the potato and tobacco to England from the New World. He first sailed to America in 1578, where, in 1585, he backed an attempt to set up a colony on Roanoke Island. On later voyages, he tried to find El Dorado, a fabled "land of gold" beyond the Orinoco River in what is now Venezuela. He had no luck, but was more successful in raiding Spanish colonies in the Caribbean.

Gold and Sugar

In the mid-sixteenth century, English explorers such as Martin Frobisher and Walter Raleigh sailed across the Atlantic Ocean seeking precious metals and spices. English **navigators** explored the coasts of North and South America and West Africa without success.

Finding no gold, the English set out to steal it from the Spanish by robbing Spanish treasure ships sailing home from South America. At the end of the sixteenth century, English **privateers** seized Spanish gold worth a huge sum every year. Such was England's control of the seas that some historians claim that in many ways the Atlantic Ocean itself can be seen as England's first "empire." English fishing ships regularly crossed the Atlantic to catch cod on the Grand Banks, sandbanks off Newfoundland.

Claiming Territory

By the early seventeeth century the English began to seize their own lands overseas. They set up colonies in Virginia and Massachusetts in North America and Antigua and Barbados in the Caribbean; they also built trading stations on the coast of India.

At home, the English acquired tastes for new luxuries, such as sugar, tea, coffee, and tobacco. Such luxuries had to be imported. Unlike the Spanish, who based their empire on gold, the British would base their empire on trade.

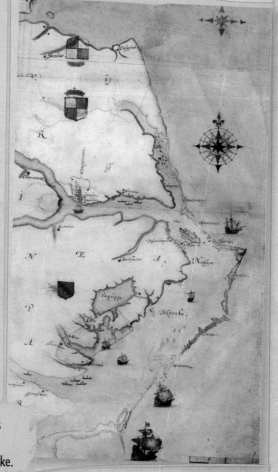

This map of the North Carolina coast was drawn by John White, governor of the short-lived first English colony on Roanoke.

The Lost Colony

In 1585, Walter Raleigh organized an attempt to settle on Roanoke Island off North Carolina in North America. The colonists soon went home but a second expedition—150 men, women, and children— arrived in 1587. Soon afterward the colonists' leader, John White, went to England for supplies. His return to Roanoke was delayed until 1590. When he returned, he found the island abandoned with no trace of the colonists. The fate of Britain's "Lost Colony" has never been explained.

Building the Empire

English colonies were formed in the Americas when settlers arrived seeking freedom to follow their own religions. About 170 years later, colonial Americans declared their independence.

This painting shows the Pilgrims sailing to North America on the *Mayflower* to find somewhere they could follow their religion.

In 1607, settlers led by Captain John Smith set up the first successful English settlement in what is now Virginia. The colony was named Jamestown, in honor of King James I (ruled 1603–1625). The colonists' wealthy backers hoped to get a return for their **investment** from trade with the colony.

On December 11, 1620, 102 mostly English settlers arrived at Plymouth, Massachusetts. Now known as the Pilgrims, many settlers were Puritans, a form of Christianity that was forbidden in England at the time. The Pilgrims wanted to create their own society beyond the religious rules of England.

William Penn meets Native Americans and European settlers as he lands in North America in 1682. The king gave Penn, a Quaker, land to start the colony of Pennsylvania.

The Population Grows

Religious freedom attracted more settlers to America. Catholics settled in Maryland in 1634, Protestants in Rhode Island in 1636, and Quakers in Pennsylvania in 1682. As the population of settlers grew, the East Coast of America was split into colonies. Most were ruled by governors on behalf of the English king. By the mid-1660s the English had also taken over small colonies established by the Swedish and Dutch. English control extended along the coast from New England in the north to the Carolinas in the south.

DAILY LIFE

Life in the New World

Life for English settlers was very hard. Many of the first arrivals had never farmed before. They struggled to grow crops for food, and many starved. Disease such as malaria was common, and there was no medicine. The colonists were suspicious of Native Americans so did not ask them for help. The two groups sometimes fought, making life even more difficult.

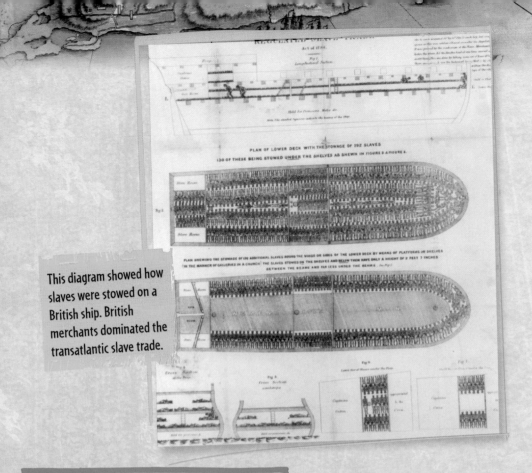

This diagram showed how slaves were stowed on a British ship. British merchants dominated the transatlantic slave trade.

Slave Trade

Sugar cultivation requires a lot of labor. English sugar growers on the Caribbean islands used slaves on their plantations to save costs. The slaves were illegally taken from West Africa and transported across the Atlantic Ocean. Some 3,100 British slave ships carried more than one million slaves. By 1790, one-quarter of Britain's income came from sugar from the West Indies.

The society of English colonies in North America was organized as it had been back in England. There were nobles and commoners. Settlers had little contact with the Native American population.

Agriculture was the main activity of the colonists. In the southern colonies, settlers grew tobacco and other export crops that required large numbers of workers. To begin with, the colonists relied on white **indentured** servants. These servants agreed to work for a certain number of years in return for the cost of their original passage to America and food and lodging when they arrived. Soon, however, the colonists began to use African slaves for labor. The first slaves arrived in Jamestown on an English warship in 1619.

Fur in Canada

The French had begun to settle in New France, now Canada, early in the 1600s. The English envied the valuable French fur trade around the Great Lakes. To challenge the French, King Charles II (ruled 1660-1685) sponsored the creation of the Hudson's Bay Company. In 1670, the company set out to create a **monopoly** on the fur trade in a vast area of northern Canada then known as Rupert's Land.

Piracy in the Caribbean

From the 1660s to the 1730s, the English were among the main pirates and privateers in the Caribbean. Some pirates had licences from the English king that allowed them to seize Spanish treasure ships. These privateers included experienced sailors such as Sir Francis Drake. They set up pirate ports in Jamaica, Haiti, and the Bahamas from which to plunder Spanish ships.

In order to trade for furs, the Hudson's Bay Company had to set up remote trading posts, like this one photographed in 1860 in Washington State.

A Dutch ship sails into Table Bay in Cape Colony in 1762. The British soon began to plan to take over the colony at the southern tip of Africa.

The Fur Trade

In 1534 the French explorer Jacques Cartier claimed Canada for France and traded with native peoples for furs. In the seventeenth century, there was a craze for fur in Europe. Initially it was used to trim coats and cloaks. Later, beaver fur was polished and made into hats. As the trade became valuable, the British set up the Hudson's Bay Company in 1670 to compete with the French.

By the mid-1700s, Britain and France between them claimed most of eastern North America. In 1754, the two powers fought a war for colonial control. British victory in the French and Indian War (1754–1763) won it much of the French territory in the New World, including Canada. The Treaty of Paris (1763) also secured Spanish Florida for Britain.

Expansion in Asia

The early English discoveries in North America had been made by explorers who were seeking a western sea route to Asia and its valuable Spice Islands. Despite the success of the American colonies, the British still wanted to find a sea route to

The East India Company

The East India Company was set up in 1600 to gain markets in Asia. Wealthy merchants owned the company and the English government had no direct control over it. Despite competing with the Dutch East India Company, the English company eventually grew so powerful it controlled half the world's trade. From 1757 until 1858, the company used its private armies to control the peoples and land of India.

Robert Clive, who worked for the East India Company, became known as "Clive of India" for his military successes in India.

Asia. They envied the huge profits the Portuguese and the Dutch were making from the spice trade.

In 1600, the British had set up the East India Company to trade across Asia. Two years later, the Dutch had set up the rival Dutch East India Company. The two rival companies competed for centuries. Unlike in North America, in India the Europeans found themselves dealing with long-established, powerful kingdoms. Northern India was ruled by the Islamic Mughal Empire. The rest of the **subcontinent** was divided into many Hindu kingdoms. The British East India Company began to set up trading posts across India.

KEY PEOPLE

Clive of India

Robert Clive (1725–1774) arrived in India as an army captain in the East India Company and ended his career as governor and commander-in-chief. After Clive's victory at the Battle of Plassey in 1757, he became governor of Bengal, while the Company took control of nearly all of India. Clive made a fortune from his achievements. He briefly returned to England in 1760 and served as a member of Parliament before becoming the first governor of India.

Control of India

To protect its trade posts, the Company, as it was known, had its own army and navy. During the seventeenth century, it used these forces against Indian rulers. After the Emperor Aurangzeb died in 1707, the power of the Mughal Empire declined and British control spread. The French also had imperial ambitions in India. In 1757, however, three thousand Company troops commanded by Captain Robert Clive defeated a French and Indian army of more than forty thousand at the Battle of Plassey. The victory gave Britain control of Bengal, one of the richest parts of India.

The Pacific Region

European sailors had crossed the Pacific since the 1500s. In the first half of the seventeenth centuries, navigators

This postcard celebrates Robert Clive's defeat of a large force of French and Indian soldiers at the Battle of Plassey in 1757.

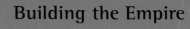

James Cook and his officers meet native people in Hawaii in the Pacific Ocean in 1778. Cook named the islands the Sandwich Islands in honor of a British noble.

discovered Australia, New Zealand, and other islands. They were too far away to be of much interest to European powers. By the middle of the eighteenth century, however, much of the known world was under European control. Seeking further expansion, the British turned their attention to the vast Pacific. Captain James Cook set sail for Tahiti in 1768. Cook's orders were to record a transit of Venus, which is when the planet passes across the face of the sun. The British were also eager to stop the French claiming land in the Pacific, however. Cook also had secret orders to **survey** the Pacific Ocean and find a way to Australia.

Cook's ship, *Endeavour*, arrived in New Zealand in 1769. He sailed around both islands of New Zealand before sailing to

KEY PEOPLE

Captain James Cook

James Cook (1728–1779) rose from humble origins to become one of the greatest of all navigators. After an apprenticeship, he joined the British Royal Navy in 1755 and charted parts of the Canadian coast during the French and Indian War. From 1766 to 1779 he led three voyages to the Pacific Ocean, making many new discoveries. He was an outstanding captain who was popular with his crew. Cook was killed in Hawaii as he tried to befriend local people.

The Problem of Longitude

A huge challenge for British sailors was to measure their position east or west on the globe, or longitude. In 1714, the British government offered a huge prize for a way to measure longitude. The prize was won by a self-taught clockmaker, John Harrison. Harrison devised a chronometer so accurate it allowed sailors to compare the time on ship to the time at home. From this, they could calculate their position in the ocean.

Australia. In April 1770, he landed at Botany Bay, which he named for its rich animal and plant life. He claimed the territory of New South Wales for Britain. The British Empire had grown even bigger.

A Mighty Loss

One reason the British wanted territory in the Pacific was because it faced rebellion on the other side of the world. The Thirteen Colonies of North America objected to their treatment by Parliament and the government in Britain. In the 1750s and 1760s, the British government imposed a series of heavy taxes on the colonies and their trade. The colonies had no members in the British Parliament who could object to the new taxes. This "taxation without representation" led to a series of protests and **boycotts** by the colonists of

British troops cross the St. Lawrence River to attack the French at Quebec in 1759, during the French and Indian War.

Massachusetts. When protestors threw British tea into Boston Harbor during the so-called Boston Tea Party in 1773, the British imposed a series of harsh new laws to punish the colonists.

In April 1775, the colonists of Massachusetts fought back. Once fighting broke out, other colonists rushed to join them. The British faced a full-scale war with their American subjects.

In July 1776, as the military campaign continued, representatives from the Thirteen Colonies declared independence from Britain. A further five years of fighting continued until the Americans eventually won a decisive victory in 1781. A peace treaty two years later confirmed Britain's loss of the Thirteen Colonies.

Canada after American Independence

Following the independence of the Thirteen Colonies from Great Britain, the colonies to the north (present-day Canada) chose to remain part of the British Empire. Quebec, Ontario, New Brunswick, and Nova Scotia remained part of the empire. In 1867, the colonies were united as the Dominion of Canada and were granted the right to run most of their own affairs.

The British commander General Lord Cornwallis surrenders at Yorktown in 1781 at the end of the American Revolution.

The Height of the Empire

In the nineteenth century, Britain added ten million square miles (sixteen million square kilometers) to its empire. By 1900, Britain ruled the largest empire the world had ever seen.

By the end of the nineteenth century, the British Empire had added vast areas of Africa and the Middle East to its colonial possessions. The empire stretched from North America to East Asia and the Pacific. At its heart, the "jewel in the crown" was India.

Controlling Trade

With colonies around the world, the British had no single formula for colonial rule. However, the basis of the empire remained trade. Colonies provided a source of raw materials for British factories as well as markets for the sale of goods

This nineteenth-century Chinese print shows officials destroying opium. The Chinese tried hard to stop the illegal trade.

manufactured in those factories. Smaller colonial outposts controlled trade routes and ports that joined the empire together.

East Asia

Opium poppies grew widely in Britain's colony in India. They produced a highly addictive drug that was popular in China. British merchants exported the drug to China. Around 1830, the price of opium fell and demand for the drug rose greatly, so the British imported more opium to China. The Chinese tried to stop them. The two sides fought the First Opium War (1839–1842). After Britain's victory, China gave Britain control of the island and port of Hong Kong.

The British now had access to Chinese markets. Chinese **exports** such as silk, tea, and porcelain were very popular in

DAILY LIFE

Dangerous Drug

The drug opium causes hallucinations and makes its users unable to move. It had been smoked in China for centuries but was very expensive. Opium poppies grew in India, so British traders began importing the drug illegally into China. By the 1830s, opium was so cheap in China that it was ruining many lives. The British ignored Chinese requests to stop the trade. The two countries fought two Opium Wars (1839–1842 and 1856–1860) before the British forced China to make the opium trade legal.

This nineteenth-century painting shows steamships in the harbor of Hong Kong, Britain's main trading port in China.

This painting shows the Battle of Trafalgar in 1805, when Britain's Royal Navy defeated a combined fleet of Spanish and French ships.

The British Royal Navy

After Lord Horatio Nelson's victory over the fleet of the Emperor Napoleon at the Battle of Trafalgar in 1805, the Royal Navy was the most powerful fleet in the world. It retained its dominance for the rest of the nineteenth century. It built faster, better-armed ships than any potential imperial rivals. That allowed it to control ocean trade and defend the outposts of the British Empire.

Britain. However, Chinese consumers wanted little from the British apart from silver and opium.

Meanwhile, the British remained jealous of Dutch colonial power in East Asia. After the French Emperor Napoleon Bonaparte took control of the Kingdom of Holland in 1811, the British targeted the Dutch East Indies in what is now Indonesia. A young employee of the East India Company, Stamford Raffles, led an attack on Java, one of the Indonesian islands. He wanted to establish a British presence in the region to challenge the Dutch. Raffles governed Java for four years before founding Bencoolen on the island of Sumatra. Finally, on February 6, 1819, the East India Company took control of an island named Singapore at the tip of the Malay Peninsula. Raffles would turn the colony into a major trading center.

Penal Colony in Australia

In Australia, the main settlers were convicts from Britain, although the first free settlers arrived in New South Wales in 1793. Soon after James Cook claimed the land for Britain, the British government began sending convicts there. Even minor crimes, such as stealing a loaf of bread, could be punished with **transportation**. Before American independence, convicts

DAILY LIFE

The First Fleet

On January 26, 1788, eleven British ships arrived in Australia with 1,500 passengers, including 751 convicted criminals. The convicts were sent to serve their sentences there to avoid overcrowding in Britain's jails. More fleets followed as convicts built jails, houses, roads, and bridges. From 1788 to 1868, when transportation ended, some 165,000 convicts were sent to Australia.

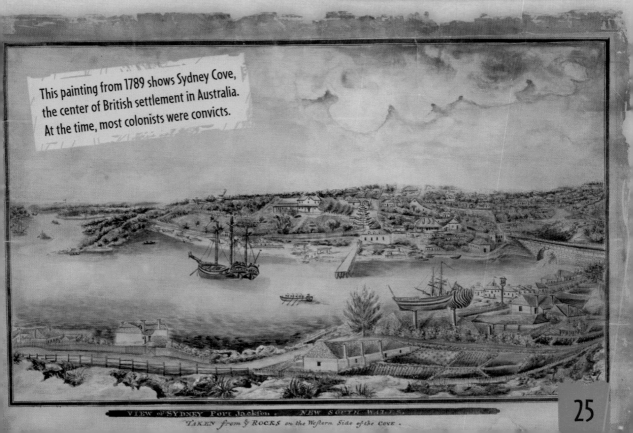

This painting from 1789 shows Sydney Cove, the center of British settlement in Australia. At the time, most colonists were convicts.

VIEW of SYDNEY Port Jackson . NEW SOUTH WALES . TAKEN from ye ROCKS on the Western Side of the COVE .

The sepoys who led the Indian Mutiny were protesting against British orders that offended their religious beliefs.

had been sent to North America, so the British needed a new destination to send them, and Australia fit the bill. The convicts would also help populate the colony. Few other settlers were willing to undertake the long voyage.

As more convicts and free settlers arrived, Europeans spread across the continent. Tasmania was founded in 1804, Western Australia in 1829, South Australia in 1836, Victoria in 1851, and Queensland in 1859. The discovery of gold in New South Wales in 1851 started a boom as settlers poured in to seek their fortunes. By 1861 the Australian population was one million. The last group of convicts arrived from Britain in 1868.

Changes in India

The middle of the century brought a profound change to India. In 1857 sepoys—Indian soldiers in the British

DAILY LIFE

Australian Gold Rush of 1851

Just three years after the Californian gold rush of 1848, Edward Hargraves struck gold in New South Wales (later part of Victoria state). Tens of thousands of prospectors flooded to Australia from around the world. These free settlers brought new skills and changed the nature of what was still mainly a penal colony. Although many prospectors did not find gold, they decided to settle. Australia's population tripled in the next twenty years from 430,000 to 1.7 million.

Army—staged a **mutiny** in northern India. They captured the capital, Delhi, and laid siege to major cities of Kanpur (Cawnpore) and Lucknow. The mutiny was defeated on July 8, 1858, but it had shocked Britain. India was removed from the control of the East India Company and ruled directly by the British government.

A viceroy was put in charge to govern on behalf of Queen Victoria, who declared herself empress of India in 1877. The period of direct rule from London was known as the British Raj, from the Hindu word for "rule." The Raj became a symbol for the glory of the British Empire in the

KEY PEOPLE

Indian Sepoys

Sepoys were native Indian soldiers in the East India Company Army. Of the army's three hundred thousand soldiers, almost 96 percent were Indian. They were vital to winning British control of India. However, they were often badly treated and had no chance of promotion because all officers were British. Resentment grew when the sepoys were forced to use a new type of rifle cartridge said to be smeared in animal fat that was forbidden to Hindus and Muslims. The angry sepoys began the Mutiny of 1857.

late nineteenth century. Elsewhere, however, the empire was having more problems imposing its rule.

The Scramble for Africa

One continent that featured relatively little in Britain's early imperial plans was Africa. Africa was seen mainly as a source of slaves to be sent to the Americas and as the location of useful supply points on the long sailing voyage to Britain's Indian colonies. As late as 1870, Europeans controlled just 10 percent of Africa; thirty years later

Queen Victoria (ruled 1837–1901) oversaw the height of Britain's power and was followed by Edward VII (ruled 1901–1910) and George V (ruled 1910–1936).

The Colonial Office

At the start of the nineteenth century, the British Empire was run by the War and Colonial Office in London. The office sent governors, district officers, secretaries, and clerks all over the world to run the colonies. As the empire grew larger, the new Colonial Office was created in 1854. When India became part of the empire, government became so complex that it had its own administrative office, the India Office.

they controlled 90 percent. The British created sixteen African colonies in the thirty years of what was known as the Scramble for Africa.

Britain's main interests in Africa were in the south, where the Cape Colony (now South Africa) controlled sea routes to India and East Asia. Cape Colony had originally been controlled by the Dutch. It was taken over by the British in 1795. Some of the colony's Dutch farmers, the Boers, trekked north to escape British rule. They formed their own colonies.

In the 1860s diamonds and gold were found in Boer territory. Thousands of Britons flooded into the region, while ambitious **adventurers** such as Cecil Rhodes planned ways in which to seize

The Battle of Isandlwana was the first time the British Army had been defeated by a technologically inferior enemy.

Boer territory. Encouraged by Rhodes, British expansion north from the Cape brought the British into conflict with the native Zulu. In January 1879, the Zulu defeated the British Army at Isandlwana. It took another six months before the Zulu were defeated and their territory absorbed into the empire.

British relations with the Boers grew worse. In 1899, the outnumbered Boers began the Boer War (1899–1902) against the British Army. Using guerrilla tactics, the Boers forced the British to make peace in 1902. The British took control of the Boer states, which became part of the Union of South Africa although the Boer states continued to manage their own affairs.

This cartoon shows Cecil Rhodes bestriding Africa. Rhodes was an adventurer who led Britain's push north from South Africa.

KEY PEOPLE

Queen Victoria

Victoria became Queen of the United Kingdom when she was just eighteen. Her long reign coincided with the rapid growth and supremacy of the British Empire.

She became Empress of India in 1877. Victoria was a passionate defender of the British Empire. As her reign continued, she became a symbol of the power of the empire itself. That made her very popular with some of her colonial subjects—but also the object of criticism by others.

The Peoples of the Empire

At its height, the British Empire ruled peoples ranging from princes in India to African slaves in the Caribbean and from French Canadians to former Dutch colonists in southern Africa.

The British Empire was at its largest by ca. 1924. About 458 million people—a quarter of Earth's population—were under British rule. Despite the loss of North America 150 years earlier, the empire had gone from strength to strength and was remarkable for its diversity.

Trade was at the root of British expansion, and the British often treated the native people of its conquered territories as little more than **commodities**. This was true for the 3.5 million Africans who were sold as slaves to work on sugar plantations in the Americas before slavery was abolished throughout the empire in 1833.

Colonies in Asia

India's 300 million people spoke many different languages, but English

The Grenadier Guards parade with their flag in 1844. The British Army offered young men the chance to serve all over the world.

was the language of government and business. The British forced Indians to grow crops for export, such as cotton and tea. This took land used for farming, and India could no longer feed all its population. A number of famines struck. Elsewhere in Asia, such as Malaysia, people worked in British-owned rubber plantations. In many ways, however, the Asian colonies kept their social structure. The British left many local rulers in place in India, as long as they acknowledged British control. They also allowed people to follow their own religions.

Aboriginal Peoples

The situation was different where British settlers clashed with indigenous, or native, peoples. In Australia, settlers fought with the Aboriginal peoples over land, which was essential to the farming on which the colonial economy depended. Between 1770 and 1920, 80 percent of Aboriginal peoples died. Some died from diseases they caught from the British, but others died in violence. On the island of

The Maharaja of Indore poses with a servant in 1877. The British left India's local rulers in place, but removed most of their power.

Aboriginal Australians

When the British first arrived, Australia was home to around half a million Aboriginal Australians. They lived in some two hundred different groups, each group with its own language. The largest group near the British colony in New South Wales was the Darug. Within three years of the colony being set up in 1788, 90 percent of the Darug had died from diseases they caught from the British, against which they had no immunity.

The Maori

The first Maori arrived in New Zealand about one thousand years ago, having sailed from islands in the Pacific Ocean. They settled along the coast, where they fished, hunted, and grew crops. By the time the first white settlers arrived, some one hundred thousand Maori lived in small groups. The Maori had no concept of land ownership. They agreed to sign the Treaty of Waitangi in 1840, giving the British control over Maori lands, but they had little understanding of the meaning of the treaty.

British men play cricket on the Caribbean island of Trinidad in 1905. Many British sports became popular in the colonies.

Tasmania, colonists fought what was called the Black War (ca. 1830) against the native inhabitants. The Aboriginal peoples were killed or driven into **exile**. They became virtually extinct on the island.

In New Zealand, the native **Maori** were weakened by divisions between tribes. They could not resist British settlement. In 1840, the Maori gave the British rights to settle on their land.

South Africa

In South Africa, meanwhile, resistance to British rule came from both the Zulu and from the Boers, who were descended from early Dutch colonists. After a bitter war, the Zulu were pushed out of British territory. The Boers tried to escape British rule by founding new colonies inland. When the British claimed those colonies, too, the Boers went to war. They lost, but their resistance ensured that the British largely left them to rule themselves.

Britons Abroad

Millions of Britons settled in colonies around the globe. The British Army needed large numbers of men to serve overseas. Many recruits came from poor backgrounds, often from Scotland or Wales. Some saw brutal fighting, but many enjoyed lives that were better than they could have had at home. Between 1815 and 1914, around ten million other Britons sailed to make new lives in colonies in Australia, South Africa, and New Zealand. Such countries developed large colonial populations. Fewer settlers made the journey to India or Africa, apart from colonial officials or business people.

Women in the Colonies

Few British women went to live in the colonies. Women did move to India in the nineteenth century, however, but in small numbers—there was one British woman for every fifty men. These women did not work. Servants did housework for them. They busied themselves with charity work and socializing. Mary Carpenter, for example, visited India in 1866 to try to help Indian women get an education.

Slaves harvest sugar cane on a plantation in the West Indies. The slave trade was abolished in the empire in 1807, and slavery itself in 1833.

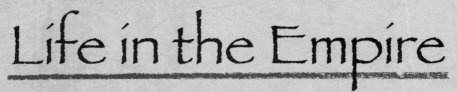

Life in the Empire

The days of the British Raj in India were the highpoint of the empire's achievements. Life in India in many ways defined the British Empire for both the British and their Indian subjects.

Although India's population was some three hundred million, it was ruled by as few as twenty thousand British men. For young British men educated at the best schools, going to India was part of a gentleman's training. It also provided him and his family with a lifestyle that was unimaginable at home. British officials lived in luxury, surrounded by servants.

An Empire Within an Empire

Most British residents had little interest in adapting to Indian ways of life. Some continued to dress in India as if they were in Britain—in dark formal suits and top hats. However, some aspects of Indian life—such as hot, spicy curries—were taken back home and introduced to Britain by former colonial residents.

British rule in India was concerned with imposing the British system of government on India. The British introduced the British legal and education systems. British engineers built telegraph networks and railroads. The construction of the

British architect Edwin Lutyens built a palace for the Viceroy of India in the new capital, New Delhi, in the 1920s.

railroads and the steam engines to run on them generated an engineering industry and formed the basis of the Indian economy. The railroads also helped to link parts of the country, making it far easier for both the British and Indians to move from region to region.

The Raj existed to make money for Britain. By the 1880s, 20 percent of Britain's total exports went to India, where the large population provided a huge market. Meanwhile, India exported textiles, spices, and tea to Britain. One of the most important resources of the Raj was people. Around 40 percent of the wealth generated by India was spent on the Indian Army. The Indian Army, which

DAILY LIFE

Hill Station at Shimla

Every summer from 1864, the British viceroy of India and his government moved to the hill town of Shimla. High in the mountains, Shimla was far cooler in the summer than down on the arid plains. Life in Shimla carried on the same, with administrative business and a busy social life. Shimla's buildings and even its rhododendrons were modeled on English life.

Shimla stands on a ridge about 7,864 feet (2,397 meters) above sea level. It was over 1,000 miles (1,600 kilometers) from the former colonial capital at Calcutta.

John Nash designed the Brighton Pavilion in the early nineteenth century as a retreat for the Prince Regent, later King George IV.

The Brighton Pavilion

Indian culture had more influence on the British than some Britons liked to admit. Indian words such as *pajama* and *bungalow* found their way into the English language, and the Indian way of drinking tea—with milk and sugar—became popular. One of the most visible Indian influences can be seen in the Royal Pavilion at Brighton, on England's southern coast. Architect John Nash mixed Indian and classical styles to create a building of marble domes and minarets.

contained both Indian and British soldiers led by British officers, formed the backbone of the empire. Its soldiers were sent all over the world. They fought with the regular British Army in the Boer War in South Africa and Indian Army soldiers served in both world wars.

Bringing England to India

For most Britons in the Raj, India's culture, religions, food, and language seemed very exotic and highly suspicious. Colonists took familiar things with them from home in addition to their clothes. They ate as they did at home, using imported tinned food, and ate in their own houses. They socialized with other British people of their own class, because colonial society was divided as in Britain. This was particularly apparent at the British clubs in India. The club was the center of life for British **expatriates**. It was where both men and women met friends to eat or drink, and to play sports such as tennis, golf, cricket, and **polo** (which had originally been introduced to the English aristocracy from Asia). For other entertainment, men would organize hunts for tigers, bears, or boars, rather than the foxes they hunted at home. Every member of the British government offices had to be able to ride a horse well, so horse riding was popular.

DAILY LIFE

The Great Exhibition

In 1851, London staged the Great Exhibition, a huge display of manufactured goods from around the British Empire. More than six million visitors—a third of Britain's population—flocked to pavilions full of goods from India, Canada, South Africa, and elsewhere. The exhibition clearly signaled the empire's position as the world's industrial leader.

A British civil servant and his young family pose at home with their servants. Even junior British employees lived well in India.

Women pick tea in the foothills of Darjeeling. The tea industry was valuable for the British, but depended on large amounts of labor.

DAILY LIFE

Sati

The British did not understand many aspects of Indian life. In particular they were horrified by the practice of sati (or suttee). Since the fourth century BCE, Hinduism had taught that if a woman's husband died she should be burned to death on the funeral pyre alongside him. The British outlawed sati in 1829 in the states they controlled directly. It was finally banned throughout India by Queen Victoria in 1861.

Domestic Servants

For British colonials, the biggest difference between life in Britain and life in India was in the home. Even the lowest-ranking British **civil servant** had Indian servants. There were servants to look after the children, to cook, to shop, to clean the house, to drive, and to tend the yard. The lifestyle of the British in India was one of comfort. The cost, however, was the risk of bad health from diseases such as malaria.

Opposition to British Rule

The British generally believed their Indian subjects were inferior to them, and in India people rebelled on a number of occasions, most significantly in 1857. The rebellions always failed because the opposition was not united. It was only in 1885 that a group of educated Indians and high-ranking British officials in India formed the Indian Congress Party. By then, many Indian middle-class men had received a British education in India and had secured jobs with the Indian Civil Service.

The men who joined the Congress Party were initially concerned with securing an Indian voice in the country's law making. Party members did not have any serious thoughts of achieving independence from Britain. That would change in the next century, however. As Europe was consumed by wars, more Indian leaders became convinced that the vast country would be better off if it governed itself.

The Imperial Durbars

The durbars were huge assemblies held in Delhi to mark the coronation of an emperor or empress of India. They were powerful displays of the wealth of the Raj. Almost every ruling Indian prince and noble attended in their royal finery, as well as thousands of VIPs. There were three durbars: in 1877 (to mark Queen Victoria becoming empress), 1903, and 1911. At the last, George V became the only British monarch to attend a durbar.

Indian princes parade with elephants at the Delhi Durbar in 1911. The durbar was one of the most extravagant displays of imperial power.

End of the Empire

By the time the British Empire had reached its greatest extent in the years after World War I (1914–1918), the British and their subjects were increasingly questioning the role of the empire.

During World War I Britain was supported by troops from its colonies in Canada, Australia, and New Zealand. The empire troops were renowned for their bravery, but many people asked why they had been drawn into a European war. In the 1920s and 1930s, people in both the colonies and Britian questioned the idea that one nation could control others in different parts of the world. In 1942, during World War II (1939–1945), the British rejected a call for independence from Mahatma Gandhi and the Indian National Congress. But with the war won and Britain broke, the British could no longer ignore Indian demands and agreed to independence.

Independence was set for August 15, 1947. The Muslim League demanded that India be **partitioned** along religious lines. The Muslims wanted a separate homeland while the Hindu majority, led by the Indian National Party, wanted to keep India together.

Muslim refugees take shelter in a camp during the partition of India. Muslims and Hindus both moved in large numbers.

MATERNITY & CHILD WELFARE

Mahatma Gandhi (center) leads a march against British rule. Gandhi's principle of nonviolent protest influenced later leaders, such as Martin Luther King.

The British agreed to create the mainly Muslim countries of West Pakistan (now Pakistan) and East Pakistan (now Bangladesh). The partition descended into bloody fighting and when the British left India the country was in chaos.

The 1950s

The loss of India seriously weakened the British Empire. Since the end of World War II it had been replaced as a global **superpower** by the United States and the Soviet Union. In an attempt to retain some global power, Britain formed the association of Commonwealth countries in 1949. This allowed colonies such as Ghana in West Africa to govern itself before gaining independence, as long as they remained within the Commonwealth.

KEY PEOPLE

Mahatma Gandhi

A trained lawyer from a wealthy Indian family, Gandhi led the movement for independence from Britain. He promoted "satyagraha," or passive resistance. He led nonviolent protests against British rule such as the 1930 Salt March against a tax on salt. Although he wanted independence, he was strongly opposed to the partition of India along religious lines. He believed Hindus and Muslims should work together. A fanatical Hindu killed Gandhi on January 30, 1948.

British soldiers consult a map during the Malayan Emergency of 1948–1960. Malayan guerrilla forces tried to drive the British out to achieve independence.

The Commonwealth

The British created the Commonwealth of Nations in 1949 as an international association of countries, most of which were formerly members of the empire. Unlike the days of the British Empire, membership of the Commonwealth is voluntary and all members are equal. The head of the Commonwealth is the reigning British monarch. There are fifty-three members of which two–Rwanda and Mozambique–were never part of the British Empire.

Seizing their opportunity, however, colonies such as Malaya, Kenya, and Cyprus revolted against British rule. The British Army faced armed uprisings in many former colonies.

In 1956, the Suez Crisis showed how weak Britain had become. Britain and France had controlled the Suez Canal in Egypt since 1869. It was a key route to India. When the Egyptians **nationalized** the canal, Britain could do nothing to stop them, despite sending troops to Egypt. It was a humiliating defeat.

The End of the Empire

During the rest of the twentieth century, British colonies gained independence and became members of the Commonwealth.

Meanwhile, Britain turned its attention to Europe, joining the European Community (now the European Union) in 1973.

The British Empire was over, but problems remained. In 1982, Britain went to war with Argentina over the Falkland Islands (Las Malvinas) in the South Atlantic. Although Britain handed Hong Kong back to China in 1997, control of the former colony continued to cause tension between Britain and China.

The Falklands War

On April 2, 1982, Argentina invaded the Falkland Islands. The group of islands in the South Atlantic Ocean, off the Argentine coast, had only 1,800 residents and had been a British colony for 150 years. A British task force sailed 8,000 miles (12,875 km) to recapture the islands after a brief war. The islands remain under British control but the Argentines continue to lay claim to them.

The British aircraft carrier HMS *Invincible* receives a heroes' welcome after returning home from the Falklands War in 1982.

Timeline

1497	John Cabot claims Newfoundland for the English king.
1587	The first English colony is founded at Roanoke, North Carolina.
1600	The East India Company is formed.
1607	Jamestown is founded in Virginia.
1614	A British colony is founded in Bermuda.
1630	Massachusetts Bay becomes a colony.
1668	The East India Company takes over Bombay.
1670	The Hudson's Bay Company is founded.
1707	The Act of Union creates the United Kingdom of Great Britain.
1713	Britain receives land in Canada after the War of the Spanish Sucession.
1754	The French and Indian War begins in North America.
1757	Robert Clive defeats France at the Battle of Plassey, leaving the British East India Company in control of most of India.
1763	The Treaty of Paris awards most of Canada to Britain.
1770	Captain James Cook claims New South Wales for Britain.
1775	The American Revolution begins; the American colonies declare independence in 1776.
1783	Britain acknowledges the independence of the Thirteen Colonies.
1788	The First Fleet arrives in New South Wales.
1795	The British seize Cape Colony from the Dutch.

1805	Nelson's victory in the Battle of Trafalgar leaves Britain in control of the world's oceans.
1819	Stamford Raffles founds Singapore off the Malay Peninsula.
1833	Slavery is abolished throughout the Empire.
1840	Treaty of Waitangi in New Zealand.
1841	A colony is established in Hong Kong, China, after the end of the First Opium War.
1857	The Indian Mutiny begins; the following year, India is taken under direct rule by the British.
1884	The Berlin Conference begins Europe's "Scramble for Africa."
1899	The Boers of southern Africa begin the Boer War, which lasts until 1902.
1910	The Union of South Africa becomes a dominion.
1914	The colonies join British forces to fight World War I.
1920	The peace conferences give the Allies temporary control in the Middle East in Iraq, Jordan, and Palestine.
1939	British and imperial forces begin fighting World War II.
1947	Partition of India and Pakistan; Britain withdraws from the Middle East.
1949	The British create the Commonwealth of Nations.
1956	The Suez Crisis demonstrates Britain's international weakness.
1982	Britain defeats Argentina in a war over ownership of the Falkland Islands.

Glossary

adventurer A person who takes risks to achieve financial or political gain.

boycotts Voluntary bans on trade with groups or countries, usually as a form of protest of punishment.

civil servant A person employed by a government to help run the affairs of a country.

commodities Raw materials that are bought and sold.

exile Being excluded from one's homeland.

expatriate A person who lives outside his or her native country.

exports Goods that are sold abroad.

imperial Related to an empire.

indentured Bound by a contract to provide labor for a certain length of time.

investment Money paid into a scheme in the hope of making more money in return.

manufactures Goods made on a large scale using machines.

Maori The indigenous people of New Zealand.

monopoly The exclusive control of trade in a particular commodity or region.

mutiny A rebellion by soldiers or sailors against their officers.

nationalized Taken from private ownership into ownership by the government.

navigators People who explore the world by sea.

partitioned Divided into parts; the phrase is used to describe the division of India into India and Pakistan.

polo A game resembling a form of hockey played on horseback.

privateers Ships with permission from a government to attack merchant ships of another country.

strategic Relating to long-term or large-scale plans.

subcontinent A large part of a continent that can be told apart from the rest.

superpower A globally powerful and influential nation.

survey To examine and record an area of land or sea for a purpose such as navigation or map-making.

transportation The practice of sending convicts to a penal colony.

Further Reading

Books

Bernard, Catherine. *The British Empire and Queen Victoria*. In World History. Berkeley Heights, NJ: Enslow Publishers, 2010.

Darraj, Susan Muaddi. *The Indian Independence Act of 1947*. Milestones in Modern World History. New York: Chelsea House Publishers, 2011.

Feinstein, Stephen. *Captain Cook: Great Explorer of the Pacific*. Great Explorers of the World. Berkeley Heights, NJ: Enslow Publishers, 2010.

Fishkin, Rebecca. *English Colonies in America*. We the People. Minneapolis, MN: Compass Point Books, 2008.

McNeese, Tim. *Colonial America 1543–1763*. Discovering US History. New York: Chelsea House Publishing, 2010.

Slavicek, Louise Chipley. *The Boer War*. Milestones in Modern World History. New York: Chelsea House Publishers, 2011.

Whitelaw, Nancy. *Queen Victoria and the British Empire*. European Queens. Greensboro, NC: Morgan Reynolds Publishing, 2005.

Websites

Atlas of the British Empire
www.atlasofbritempire.com
An interactive atlas of the British Empire at different periods.

British National Archives
www.nationalarchives.gov.uk/education/empire

The history of the empire from the British National Archives.

History.com
www.history.com/topics/british-history
History.com index of British history, with links to pages about the empire.

Publisher's note to educators and parents: Our editors have carefully reviewed these websites to ensure that they are suitable for students. Many websites change frequently, however, and we cannot guarantee that a site's future contents will continue to meet our high standards of quality and educational value. Be advised that students should be closely supervised whenever they access the Internet.

Index